*I Want
to Laugh ,*

*I Want
to Cry*

Other books by

Blue Mountain Press INC.

Come Into the Mountains, Dear Friend
by Susan Polis Schutz
Peace Flows from the Sky
by Susan Polis Schutz
Someone Else to Love
by Susan Polis Schutz
I'm Not That Kind of Girl
by Susan Polis Schutz
Yours If You Ask
by Susan Polis Schutz

The Best Is Yet to Be
Step to the Music You Hear, Vol. I
The Language of Friendship
The Language of Love
The Language of Happiness
The Desiderata of Happiness
by Max Ehrmann
Whatever Is, Is Best
by Ella Wheeler Wilcox
Poor Richard's Quotations
by Benjamin Franklin
I Care About Your Happiness
by Kahlil Gibran/Mary Haskell
My Life and Love Are One
by Vincent Van Gogh
I Wish You Good Spaces
by Gordon Lightfoot
We Are All Children Searching for Love
by Leonard Nimoy
Catch Me with Your Smile
by Peter McWilliams
Creeds to Love and Live By

I Want
to Laugh,

I Want
to Cry

Poems on women's feelings
by
Susan Polis Schutz

Designed and illustrated
by Stephen Schutz

Blue Mountain Press ™.

Boulder, Colorado

The following poems have appeared earlier:
"Your heart is my heart," Copyright © Continental
Publications, 1971.
"The ocean brought me peace," Copyright ©
Continental Publications, 1971.

Library of Congress Number: 73-83407
ISBN : 0-88396-002-8

Manufactured in the United States of America

First Printing: October, 1973
Second Printing: January, 1974
Third Printing: January, 1975
Fourth Printing: November, 1975
Fifth Printing: January, 1977
Sixth Printing: May, 1978

Blue Mountain Press INC.

P.O. Box 4549, Boulder, Colorado 80306

CONTENTS

7   Introduction

I WANT TO LAUGH

11   You are mine
13   Music touches feelings
14   Your heart is my heart
15   When lying beside you
17   I am so happy with you
18   Thunder, lightning
19   Today we celebrated
20   Don't ever say wife to me
21   Those in love
23   I sit here
25   It's nighttime
27   Someone
29   Today I woke up
31   Thanks, Mom
33   The ocean brought me peace

I WANT TO CRY

37   You want the kind of girl who
39   The New Woman
41   When I become a young mother
43   Do It Now Sister
45   I see a little boy being bullied by bigger boys
47   Men are told by society that
48   An Education?
49   Baby Girl Gets It From All Ends
51   I don't want to be a Bookkeeper
52   I want to do
53   What kind of person am I
55   I am a city woman
57   I stare out my window
59   I stare at the sky
61   I want to laugh

62   About the Authors

INTRODUCTION

Many people argue that reason should guide all that we do and think, and that feelings are a weakness. This attitude is an attempt to hide our inner selves so that we remain unknown.

I believe that we should cultivate and show our feelings, for they are what make us unique and sensitive human beings. Families are started because of feelings. Artists create because of feelings. The feeling of love towards each other could be strong enough to stop wars.

If every decision would reflect our feelings as well as our reason, the world would be a better place to live.

I Want to Laugh, *I Want to Cry* is a way of expressing some of my feelings on paper.

Thank you for listening.

S.P.S.

I Want
to Laugh

You are mine
and I am yours
in love

I am I
and you are you
in thought

Independently
we share our lives
together

Music touches feelings
that words can not.
It is the melody
of the heart,
the voice
of the Spirit.
It inspires some
to think of the past,
some to create
and some to cry.

Music makes me
love.

Your heart is my heart
your truth is my truth
your feeling is my feeling

But the real strength of our love
is that we share rather than
control each other's lives

When lying beside you
it is strange and away from reality.
I am surrounded by flowers, and you
are all that nature is.

I am so happy with you
I can discuss all my thoughts, or
I don't have to say anything
You always understand.

I am so relaxed with you
I don't need to pretend
I don't need to look good
You accept me for what I am.

I am so strong with you
I depend on you for love
but I live my own life
You give me extra confidence to succeed.

Thunder, lightning
sun is gone; clouds are red
ground is fed

Clouds disappear
land is dry
rainbowed sky

Today we celebrated
the birthday of our love.
We rode our motorcycle
down an old dirt road
on the side of a still pure lake.
The clouds touched our heads
on the long bumpy cliff.
Twenty miles away from life
we stopped.

Seven years ago we met.
Six years ago we loved.
And now, still, we love more.
Our bodies met
outside in the sand.
The air sent a chill
to wake us
from our fantasy.
Us
the sun
the lake
the sand
forever.

Don't ever say wife to me
it's too cold
if someone asks who I am
tell them I am the one you love
if they quiver, "Are you married?"
then say that we are sharing our lives together

Those in love
must remain complete people
first unto themselves
and then to each other

I sit here
bored
I don't feel like talking
to the people here
I don't feel like looking
at this place anymore

I sit here
lonely
realizing that it's not
people or places that
make me happy
It's you

It's nighttime
I see your face
in the stars
I feel your gentleness
with the swaying of the leaves

It's nighttime
cold and dark
but the moon
warms my heart
with the thought
that we will
be together again soon

Someone
to talk with
to dance with
to sing with
to eat with
to laugh with
to cry with
to think with
to understand
Someone
to be my friend

Today I woke up
feeling strange
but special.
For the first time
in my life,
I thought about the fact that I
could produce a baby.
Out of me,
from he,
a little baby.
Unbelievable.

Sure, all my friends
have had babies,
but I never thought of myself
as a man's wife
or a child's mother.
I am just me, leading
my own life
and in love with he.

But today I pictured
a little baby building sand castles,
and it belonged to us.

THANKS, MOM

Since I had a mother
whose many interests
kept her excited and occupied

Since I had a mother
who interacted with so many people
that she had a real feeling for the world

Since I had a mother
who always was strong
through any period of suffering

Since I had a mother
who was a complete person
I always had a model
to look up to
and that made it easier
for me to develop into
an independent woman

The ocean brought me peace
the wind gave me energy
the sun warmed my spirit
the flowers showed me life
but you made me feel
                    love

I Want
to Cry

You want the kind of girl who
fixes your clothes
cooks your food
and cleans your house
while waiting for you to
come home from work

You want the kind of girl
who your friends will call fun
and your boss will call pretty
and who you may call your very own

You want the kind of girl
who looks and feels perfect
who admires you
and who listens to you in awe

You want the kind of girl
who gives up her career
to help you succeed in yours
and who gives up her whole being
to make you a superman

Well honey
I'm proud to say that
I'm not that kind of girl

THE NEW WOMAN

The new woman arises
full of confidence
she speaks eloquently
and thinks independently

Full of strength
she organizes efficiently
and directs proudly

She is the new woman
capable of changing
the course
of society

When I become a young mother,
will my life be centered in the kitchen?
Will I listen to the day's activities of my family
and have nothing to say about mine?
Will I dream about a career I could have had?
Will I lose my creativity and become bored with life?
When I become a young mother,
why can't I live the life I did before?

DO IT NOW SISTER

After my babies grow up, I'm going to
grow my hair long again
and buy new clothes for myself.
I'm going to go to Europe
and meet all kinds of people.
I'm going to go back to school
and finish my degree.
I'm going to start my career in
social work.
I used to want all these things
before I had my babies.
After my children grow up,
I'll become a person again.

I see a little boy being bullied by bigger boys
tears come to my eyes
I see New York City with all its action
and I get so excited that I stammer
I smell rubbing alcohol which reminds me of hospitals
and I cry for all the sick people
I meet people whom I love
and I love them openly
I am so glad that I have learned not to
hide my feelings

Men are told by society that
they always have to be strong
and put on a tough exterior
to block out all sensitive "unmanly" feelings

It is drilled into men from birth
that they are leaders
that they must achieve
that they must succeed in a career
Men are judged their whole lives
by the power they have
and how much they earn

I would hate to have
such overwhelming pressure
threaten my entire life

AN EDUCATION?

"What do you want to be when you grow up?"
the teacher asked her pupils.
"A fireman," Nelson answered.
"A policeman," yelled Robert.
"A nurse," said Myra.
"A baseball player," shouted Michael.
"A mother," answered Sonia.
"An airplane pilot," whispered Baby girl.

Everyone in the class laughed at Baby girl.
"Did you ever see a girl pilot?" yelled Bob.
"Well it is possible. All I have to do is
learn to fly real well," defended Baby girl.
"Girls aren't supposed to fly airplanes. Only
boys are pilots; right, teacher?" asked Mike.
"Well boys and girls, I must admit that I
have never seen a woman airplane pilot. Didn't
you once say that you wanted to be a teacher,
Baby girl?" asked the teacher.
"No, I always wanted to be a pilot,"
claimed Baby girl.
"See Baby girl," the teacher sermonized,
"most girls work only a few years after they
are done with school. Then they get married
and spend all their time raising a family."
"Yeah, girls are too stupid to be airplane
pilots," shouted Nelson.
"Well how come I get all A's, and you get
all C's?" asked Baby girl proudly.

BABY GIRL GETS IT FROM ALL ENDS

Baby girl is born!
Pink pajamas,
Pink booties,
and a pink bonnet
to make her look like
a sweet little princess.

Baby girl's fifth birthday,
and lots of dolls,
and doll clothes,
and little furniture
for Baby girl's doll house.
"Of course she likes these toys,
and besides, it's good training for
later in life."

Baby girl's knees keep getting bruised
and she asks to be allowed to wear
slacks to school.
Mother says, "Of course not.
No other girl does, and if
you'd stop being a tomboy, you wouldn't
keep falling. It almost serves you right."
"What is a tomboy?" Baby girl asks her mother.
"It's a girl who likes boy's games rather than girl's games,"
answers Mother.
"What's a boy's game?" Baby girl queries.
"Climbing trees, football, you know, anything wild."
" I want to play exciting games like the boys do,"
Baby girl yells.
"They wouldn't even let you play because you're much
weaker than they are," assured mother.
"No I'm not. Today I beat up Michael, and he's the
strongest boy in the class!" said Baby girl proudly.

I don't want to be a Secretary
I should be a President

I don't want to be a Bookkeeper
I should be the Accountant

I don't want to be a Gal Friday
I should be the General Manager

I don't want to be a Saleswoman
I should be the Marketing Manager

I don't want to be a Switchboard Operator
I should be the Communications Coordinator

Instead of being an Assembly Checker
I ought to be the Quality Control Technician

Instead of being an Alteration Lady
I ought to be a Tailor

Instead of being a Midwife
I ought to be an Obstetrician

Instead of being a Cook
I ought to be a Chef

I don't want to be a Secretary
I should be a President

I want to do
what I want to do
I want to be
what I want to be

What kind of person am I?
Am I good?
Am I kind?
Am I honest?
Am I loving?
Do I have talents?
Am I smart?
You should judge me on
these things;
but, that I am a woman
tells you nothing.

I am a
city woman,
aggressive and independent.
I wear the latest fashions
to my Broadway office.
I romance with
actors, lawyers, and executives;
I've been with many men.
I see my psychoanalyst once a week;
and if I have spare time,
I go to art museums and read the New York Times.
I eat out
and sleep five hours a night.
I move very fast
and every minute of my day and night is occupied.
I am a
city woman
who dreams a lot
about the country.

I stare out my window
and 10,000 windows stare back
families, lovers, roommates in each apartment
involved in their own fictions

Lights blinking — airplanes, bridges, cars
everyone is running
you cannot even see the stars.

I wonder who lives in the window
with the flowers
and what are they thinking
as they gaze through their glass

How can I stand out so as
not to be just another
window shadow?

I stare at the sky
and wonder why
why have we made such a mess of things

How could we tear up the seas
use up all the trees
all in the name of progress

I close my eyes
my love and I
with dreams of flowers and trees
admiring the leaves
nature is beautiful
love is ecstatic

Now is the time to
enjoy these things

I want to laugh
I want to cry

I am aggressive
I am shy

I feel strong
I feel weak

I feel confident
I feel meek

I look pretty
I look bad

I feel happy
I feel sad

I am love
I am hate

I act crazy
I act straight

I feel soft
I feel tough

I feel sexy
I feel rough

Many emotions amidst each day
together with reason are what guide my way

ABOUT THE AUTHORS

Susan and Stephen are the best-selling poet-artist team in the United States. Their first six books, Come Into the Mountains, Dear Friend; I Want to Laugh, I Want to Cry; Peace Flows from the Sky; Someone Else to Love; I'm Not That Kind of Girl; and Yours If You Ask, are continual bestsellers, with combined sales of well over one million copies. In addition, their poetry and illustrations have appeared on over 50 million notecards and prints, and have drawn exceptional response from numerous readers.

After attending graduate school, Susan worked as a teacher, a social worker and a newspaper reporter. In addition to writing six poetry books and editing a variety of others, she has had many articles published in magazines and newspapers and is working on an autobiographical novel.

Stephen studied at the New York High School of Music and Art, the Boston Museum of Fine Arts School, the Massachusetts Institute of Technology, and received a Ph.D. from Princeton University in 1970. Stephen, who has designed and illustrated all of Susan's books, is well known for his original calligraphy, serigraph techniques and airbrush paintings.